LONDON MURDER STORIES

RECALLING THE EVENTS OF SOME OF LONDON'S MOST
FASCINATING MURDERS

Brian Langston

BRADWELL
BOOKS

Published by Bradwell Books

9 Orgreave Close Sheffield S13 9NP

Email: books@bradwellbooks.co.uk

British Library Cataloguing in Publication Data: a catalogue
record for this book is available from the British Library.

1st Edition

ISBN: 9781910551769

Print: Gomer Press, Llandysul, Ceredigion SA44 4JL

Artwork by: Andrew Caffrey

Photograph Credits: Creative Commons
or credited individually

CONTENTS

INTRODUCTION

Murder is the most monstrous of crimes and yet few could deny that it grips us with a macabre fascination.

During my thirty-year career as a police officer, I have had the misfortune to encounter many murderers, including East End gangster Ronnie Kray and 'Yorkshire Ripper' Peter Sutcliffe. I have also witnessed radical advancements in technology and forensic science which now make it extremely unlikely that a murderer will escape detection. However, in this enthralling selection of London Murder Stories, the Metropolis was a very different place. In a world long before CCTV and DNA, and when the penalty for murder was death, the greatest assets to crime investigation were often the copper's instinct and the nosey neighbour.

A whole library has been devoted to London's most notorious murderer, Jack the Ripper, so his diabolical crimes are not discussed in depth here, although his malign influence inspired at least one of the killers in this book. And at Miller's Court, Whitechapel, the very house in which he perpetrated his most atrocious attack, another victim was brutally slain a decade later.

This collection of twelve gruesome murders spanning two and a half centuries begins in the bustling coffee shops of the Stuarts and moves to the graceful squares of the Georgians before progressing to the foggy Victorian cobbled streets and culminates in the bombed-out austerity of post-war London.

So sit back and enjoy this murderous journey from the wretched slums of Whitechapel to the elegant mansions of Kensington, where old-fashioned detective work was aided, on at least one occasion, by supernatural agency, and in another case by dogged canine determination.

Brian Langston Q.P.M.

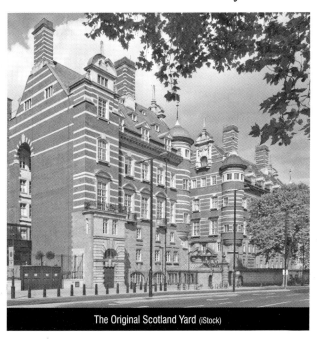

The Original Scotland Yard (iStock)

house near St Paul's churchyard. At nine o'clock in the evening on Monday 4 January 1692, two men hailed a cab at the Fetter Lane end of Fleet Street and asked the coachman, Mr Sikes, to take them to Dr Clenche's house in Brownlow Street. On arrival they told him to go and fetch the doctor to attend to a patient who was seriously ill. Mr Sikes duly obliged, finding the doctor in his nightclothes on his way to bed. He quickly dressed and climbed into the waiting carriage containing the two mysterious strangers. He was never seen alive again. Sikes was asked to drive to Leadenhall Market and then urged to race at high speed to the Pye Tavern in Aldgate and then back to Leadenhall Market, where they gave him three shillings and sixpence and sent him to fetch two chickens from a poulterer called Hunt, which the bemused cabbie did. When he finally returned to his cab at 10.30pm, he found the two men had gone.

On looking into his carriage he found the doctor sitting on the floor of the carriage slumped to one side. Thinking he might be drunk, he summoned a Constable of the Watch, who discovered the handkerchief ligature around his neck containing a piece of coal, pulled tight against his windpipe. His lifeless body was taken to the Bull Tavern nearby, where he was bled from both arms in an effort to revive him but was pronounced dead. His silver ink-horn and other valuables were still in his pocket, showing that robbery was not the motive.

It was no secret that Captain Harrison wished him ill and he was quickly traced and arrested. At his trial at the Old Bailey on Wednesday 6 April, Harrison, who had previously worked at the Inns of Court, chose to defend himself, denying all knowledge of the murder. His alibi, however, was quickly proved to be a sham and a succession of witnesses testified that they had overheard him threatening to cut the throat of Dr Clenche whilst in conversation with Mrs Vanwicke in Joe's Coffee House, in Holborn. Many suggested Harrison had gambled away Mrs Vanwicke's inheritance and was the cause of her financial problems rather than her saviour. Damningly, the handkerchief which was found around the doctor's throat was identified as the same one seen drying in front of the fire at Mrs Garway's lodgings.

The jury took just 30 minutes to find Harrison guilty and he was sentenced to death. He protested his innocence to the end and was hanged at Newgate on Friday 15 April 1692.

In an extraordinary twist in September of that year, John Cole was arrested and charged with being an accomplice in the murder. However, during his trial Mrs Mary Milward came forward and stunned the court with a remarkable announcement. She said that just before his death, her recently deceased husband, John Milward, had admitted murdering Dr Clenche with John Cole. Furthermore, she claimed her husband's ghost had plagued her to come forward and make the confession on his behalf. Whilst the judge cautioned that the evidence was unreliable, the jury was thrown into a state of confusion. Using twisted logic, they reasoned that as Harrison had already been executed as the killer, Cole could not be guilty if Milward was posthumously claiming to be the second killer! Despite a complete lack of corroboration, Mrs Milward's bizarre testimony placed sufficient doubt in the mind of the jury, and John Cole walked from the court a free man.

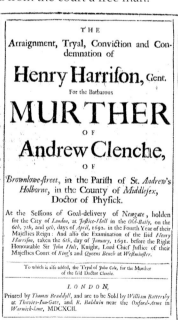

THE

Arraignment, Tryal, Conviction and Con-
demnation of

Henry Harrifon, Gent.

For the Barbarous

MURTHER

OF

Andrew Clenche,

OF

Brownlowe-ftreet, in the Parifh of St. *Andrew's
Holborne*, in the County of *Middlefex*,
Doctor of Phyfick.

At the Seffions of Goal-delivery of *Newgate*, holden
for the City of *London*, at *Juftice-Hall* in the *Old-Baily*, on the
6th, 7th, and 9th, days of *April*, 1692. in the Fourth Year of their
Majefties Reign : And alfo the Examination of the faid *Henry
Harrifon*, taken the 6th. day of *January*, 1691. before the Right
Honourable Sir *John Holt*, Knight, Lord Chief Juftice of their
Majefties Court of *King's* and Queens Bench at *Weftminfter*.

To which is alfo added, the Tryal of *John Cole*, for the Murder
of the faid Doctor *Clenche*.

LONDON,

Printed by *Thomas Braddyll*, and are to be Sold by *William Battersby*
at *Thavies-Inn-Gate*, and *R. Baldwin* near the *Oxford-Arms* in
Warwick-lane, MDCXCII.

1691 Pamphlet of Henry Harrison's Trial

MURDER IN MINIATURE

THEODORE GARDELLE 1761

THEODORE GARDELLE WAS A SWISS-BORN ARTIST WHO HAD BEGUN TO DEVELOP A REPUTATION AS A TALENTED MINIATURIST WHEN HE LEFT HIS WIFE AND TWO CHILDREN BEHIND IN PARIS AND MOVED TO GEORGIAN LONDON TO FURTHER HIS CAREER. HE LODGED ON THE SECOND FLOOR OF THE HOME OF MRS ANNE KING IN LEICESTER SQUARE. SHE WAS DESCRIBED AS A SHOWY WOMAN OF DUBIOUS CHARACTER WITH MANY GENTLEMEN CALLERS.

On Thursday 19 February 1761, Gardelle ordered Mrs King's young maidservant, Nanny, to post a letter to Mr Mozier in the Haymarket and to bring him back a pennyworth of snuff from the tobacconist next door. When she reported the request to her mistress, Mrs King complained that there would be no one in the house to answer the door if anyone called while she was out. Nanny then told Gardelle that if he could come downstairs to keep an eye on the door, she could run the errand, which he duly did.

According to Gardelle's later confession, he was sitting in the parlour awaiting the maid's return when Mrs King called out from her bedroom and began to berate him about the poor quality of the miniature portrait he had painted of her. An argument ensued and, in his poor English, Gardelle called her an impertinent woman, which enraged her further, and she punched him with a violent blow to the chest. He responded by pushing her backwards, causing her to trip on a carpet, and she fell into the bedroom, banging her head on a bed post with great force. Dazed by the fall and bleeding heavily she began to shout at Gardelle. He attempted to staunch the bleeding but she threatened to have him arrested for attacking her. He became furious and, picking up a long-handled ivory comb, in a fit of rage he plunged the handle into her throat to silence her. She died in a pool of blood in his arms. In a state of panic Gardelle bundled the body up in the bed sheets to prevent the blood from running into the hallway then, aghast at what he had done, he collapsed in a faint. When he awoke he could hear the maid, who had returned with his snuff, cleaning elsewhere in the house.

Gardelle quickly ran upstairs and changed out of his blood-soaked clothing, and stashed it away in his bureau. He sent the maid out on an errand to post another letter and whilst she was out, he stripped Mrs King's corpse of her bloodstained clothing and hid it under his bed. He then soaked the bloodied bed sheets in a water butt in the wash house.

When Nanny returned a short time later she noticed that he appeared agitated and was told that her mistress had gone out with a gentleman. The maid suspected this was a lie, and throughout the afternoon her suspicions grew when she saw Gardelle making surreptitious trips up and down stairs. Gardelle realised that he needed to get rid of the inquisitive maid permanently and hatched a plot to dismiss her. Knowing the maid could not read or write, he faked a letter of dismissal from Mrs King, paid her wages and sent her on her way.

Thomas Pelsey, a footman of another resident, who was away in the country, then came back to the house and enquired about Mrs King, and was told that she had gone out. It was not until 7pm that evening that Gardelle was alone in the house and could begin the gruesome task of disposing of the body.

On Saturday, two days after the murder, Mr Mozier, who had been with Mrs King the day before she was killed, called to take her to the opera. He was told by Gardelle that she had suddenly gone to Bristol or Bath. Mr Mozier noticed Gardelle seemed out of sorts and, assuming he was missing female company, called back later with a 'girl of the town', Sarah Walker, to look after him and help clean the house in the absence of a maid. Gardelle reluctantly accepted the offer to avoid raising any suspicion, but was thereafter frustrated by her constant attentions, finding it impossible to dispose of the body.

The following morning Gardelle rose early and left his new companion in bed. She came down three hours later and found him lighting the fire. After breakfast he sent her out to find a charwoman and she returned with Mrs Pritchard. After several days Mrs Pritchard and the footman Tom Pelsey began to suspect something was amiss. A foul smell was emanating from Mrs King's bedroom. When asked what it was, Gardelle told them that it was just the smell of bones that someone had burnt in the fire.

That night, when the rest of the house was asleep, Gardelle cut the corpse of Mrs King into pieces, throwing the bowels into the toilet pit and hiding lumps of flesh in the cockloft, where he thought they would putrefy and dry without attracting attention. On the Wednesday evening he dismissed Sarah Walker, telling her that Mrs King was due back that night, but the footman and charwoman remained in the house. When the water in the cistern failed, Mrs Pritchard went to draw some from the tub in the back kitchen, where she discovered the bloodstained bedclothes from Mrs King's bed. When Mr Pelsey's employer returned from the country he was told of the suspicious activity and constables were sent to Leicester Square to investigate.

The artist strenuously denied anything was wrong but on being questioned fell into another faint. Finding the bedroom door locked, the Bow Street Runners broke in through a window and discovered the blood-drenched bed but no trace of Mrs King. Gardelle was arrested on suspicion of her murder.

Upon searching the house they discovered the incriminating bloody linen secreted around the house. Gardelle stuck to his story, confident that the body would not be found. In the meantime builders had been sent in to search for the body and uncovered Mrs King's grisly remains scattered all around the house. In the cockloft at the top of the house they found one of her breasts and other viscera. In the toilet they found her entrails and, in the garret fireplace, her partially burnt bones.

The case was strengthened further when an enamel painter called Perroneau came forward saying that Gardelle had entrusted him with a box which he said contained precious paints, but when he heard of his arrest he had opened it and found it contained Mrs King's watch and other valuables.

Whilst in New Prison, Clerkenwell, awaiting trial Gardelle took an overdose of opium in an attempt to commit suicide. When this failed to kill him, he swallowed twelve copper coins which again had no adverse effect on his health. He was brought to trial at the Old Bailey on Thursday 2 April 1761.

He admitted the crime and when asked why he had not fled, answered that he feared another innocent person might be charged with the murder. He was found guilty of the murder of Anne King and sentenced to death. On Saturday 4 April the cart carrying him to the scaffold stopped briefly outside the spot where he had committed the murder and he was taken to the Haymarket where he was hanged in front of an enormous crowd who bayed for his blood. His corpse was then gibbeted in chains on Hounslow Heath until it decayed, to serve as a warning to other would-be murderers.

Wale Delin

Record sculp!

Theodore Gardelle having murdered M.ʳˢ King burns some parts of her Body & hides the rest

Gardelle disposing of the remains of Mrs King

BLOODSHED IN BELGRAVIA

WILLIAM JOHN MARCHANT 1839

TWO YEARS INTO THE REIGN OF QUEEN VICTORIA, LONDON WAS STUNNED BY THE HORRIFIC MURDER OF A YOUNG SERVANT GIRL, BY AN 18-YEAR-OLD FOOTMAN, WILLIAM JOHN MARCHANT.

Marchant was servant to Henry Edgell, the county magistrate for Chelsea, who lived at the prestigious five-storey Belgravia address of 21 Cadogan Place in Sloane Street. He joined the staff seven months before the tragic murder and quickly settled into the below-stairs team, becoming popular with both his employers and colleagues alike. A month later, attractive and flirtatious 19-year-old Elizabeth Ann Paynton from Oxfordshire arrived as under-housemaid.

On Friday 17 May 1839, whilst the family were away in the country, spirits were high and the atmosphere was very relaxed in the servants' hall as Ann playfully flashed her garters, much to the amusement of her fellow servants and to the embarrassment of William Marchant. At 3.30pm the housekeeper Elizabeth Gough and cook Elizabeth Strike went into town, leaving William and Ann in the house alone. As the cook left, she jokingly challenged the bashful footman to get one of Ann's garters before she returned, and said that if he didn't there would be a penalty to pay.

William helped Ann to finish her chores but the sexual banter continued and at some point crossed the line. The affronted housemaid slapped his face and told him she would get him dismissed for his rudeness. Exactly what happened next remains a mystery, but appears to have been completely out of character for young Marchant. He left the drawing room and came back with a cut-throat razor which he said he was going to use to cut off her garters. She warned him not to come anywhere near her and then, after a brief struggle in which she resisted his advances, in an inexplicable impulse he slashed her neck wide open. She fell immediately to the floor, writhing in agony with blood gurgling from a gaping throat wound.

Marchant looked down in horror at what he had done. He later said that he had not the least intention of harming her and yet, in a moment of insanity, he had inflicted a brutal and fatal injury upon his friend. He threw the razor to the floor and fell to his knees clutching the convulsing body of Ann as she gasped her last breath, their bodies saturated in a crimson tide of blood. He sobbed and prayed for several minutes, holding her limp body close to his chest. Then the full dreadfulness of his crime dawned upon him. He ran out into the hallway, put on his greatcoat to cover his blood-soaked clothing, and fled in panic into the crowded streets of Chelsea.

William Marchant murdering Eliza Paynton

When the cook and housekeeper returned to the house at 6pm that night, they found the house locked, in complete darkness and eerily silent. After getting the coachman to break in through the back door, a candlelit search of the house was made but there was no sign of either William Marchant or Ann Paynton. The housekeeper then entered the drawing room and saw a figure lying on the floor near the window. Believing she had found the couple up to no good, she furiously strode over, calling out, 'You wretch – what have you been up to?' She nudged the body with her foot and screamed out in horror as she caught sight of the appalling gash across Ann's throat: 'Oh my God! Here's Ann with her throat cut!'

The other servants rushed into the drawing room and found the dead body of their colleague lying in a pool of congealed blood with a cut-throat razor and her maid's cap lying nearby. In her right hand she grasped some hair. On her left hand there appeared to be defence wounds. One shoe was off, her stockings were pulled down and her garters were gone. There was evidence of a violent struggle having taken place in the room but no sign of William Marchant. Despite strong circumstantial evidence of a murder having been committed, the attending surgeon declared it was a case of suicide!

Meanwhile William Marchant fled across London to Windsor, where he took at room at the Two Brewers, a stone's throw from Windsor Castle. Throughout the night he was haunted by the anguished spectre of the murdered housemaid urging him to give himself up. On Sunday morning, tired and desperate, he attended a church service at Eton College Chapel and prayed for forgiveness, but as he opened his eyes, there sitting next to him on the pew was the bloodied ghost of young Ann, glaring at him accusingly.

Unable to bear the torment any longer, he walked back towards London and gave himself up to Inspector William Lawrence of the Hounslow Horse Patrol. The dishevelled youth dressed in a drab greatcoat, buttoned up to his chin, confessed to having murdered the young servant girl in Belgravia two days previously. Inspector Lawrence could scarcely believe what he was being told. Sensing the officer's scepticism, Marchant opened his coat and showed him his bloodstained livery. 'This is her blood,' he said calmly.

Marchant was taken to Old Brentford police station but throughout the journey unnerved his escort as he cowered with fear, pointing behind him and shouting, 'See her? There she is again! The girl I killed. She has been haunting me all day.' In an attempt to reassure his nervous prisoner the officer said, 'Perhaps she is not dead?' 'Oh I know she is dead for certain, sir', replied Marchant, 'for I cut her throat in three places.'

The following morning he appeared at the inquest which was held at the Bedford Arms in Pont Street, Chelsea. The streets were thronged with baying crowds eager to catch a glimpse of the monster who had so brutally murdered poor Ann Paynton.

The Coroner took the jurors to the scene of the crime where, two days after its discovery, the body of Ann Paynton remained in situ in the Belgravia drawing room.

And **JOHN MARCHENT**, for the Wilful Murder, Committed upon the body of Anne Paynton, Aged 20, at No. 21, Cadogan-place, Sloane-street, Chelsea.

William Marchant in Court

There, in front of the horror-struck jury, the clothing was cut away from the corpse and a crude forensic examination of the young servant's body was conducted. The full extent of her injuries was then revealed. There had indeed been three incisions across her throat; one was superficial but the others were eight inches long and had fatally severed her carotid artery and jugular vein. This was clearly a case of homicide and not suicide.

During the inquest, William Marchant collapsed with remorse and had to be revived. The jury, swayed by a lack of evidence of motive or premeditation, initially failed to agree, believing it to be a case of manslaughter carried out in the heat of the moment. The Coroner, however, was of a different view, citing the procurement of a razor as evidence of 'malice aforethought', and eventually a unanimous verdict of murder was returned and he was committed for trial.

The nocturnal visitations of the dead servant plagued him in his cell until his trial at the Old Bailey on Friday June 21 1839, when Marchant pleaded guilty, telling the judge that he would not lie simply to save his life. His bitter regret and wretched appearance invoked the pity of all those present, but the judge showed no mercy and, donning the black cap, passed the sentence of death.

At 8am on Monday 8 July 1839, the prison bell at the Old Bailey began to toll its mournful peal and William Marchant was removed from the condemned cell at Newgate and taken to the scaffold where, in front of a crowd of hundreds of spectators, he was hanged. The hangman botched the job, however, not allowing sufficient fall to break his neck, and the young servant died a slow and agonising death, kicking frantically in mid-air for several minutes before finally choking to death. At midnight, the teenage murderer, driven to confess by the ghost of his victim, was buried in the confines of Newgate prison yard.

THE BRYANSTON SQUARE MURDER

MARY ANN HUNT 1847

ON WEDNESDAY 2 JUNE 1847 PC CHARLES BATTERSBY
WAS PATROLLING THE QUIET STREETS OF BRYANSTON
SQUARE IN THE CITY OF LONDON, WHEN HIS ATTENTION
WAS DRAWN TO A YOUNG WOMAN ON THE DOORSTEP
OF 40 ADAM STREET WEST (NOW SEYMOUR PLACE). IT
WAS 4.30AM AND THE WOMAN WAS EMERGING FROM
THE HOUSE WITH TWO HEAVY BUNDLES. AS SHE SAW THE
POLICEMAN SHE RETREATED BACK INTO THE HOUSE AND
CLOSED THE DOOR.

Thinking this was suspicious, the diligent constable kept
watch from a doorway. His patience was rewarded when
45 minutes later the door was seen to slowly open and the
young woman appeared again briefly before disappearing
back into the house. PC Battersby went across to investigate
and, finding the door ajar, pushed it open to find Mary Ann
Hunt standing there with the two bundles on the floor
beside her. Mary Ann was an unemployed servant who
lived at the house with an elderly friend, with whom she
had previously been in service.

He then asked why she was acting so suspiciously and Mary Ann gave a furtive response and told him to take the parcels if he wanted. PC Battersby said he was going nowhere until he had seen the lady of the house. Mary Ann said, 'I suppose it's no use telling you a lie,' and showed him into a room entirely devoid of furniture in which she claimed she lived with Mrs Mary Stowell.

Making enquiries of another lodger, PC Battersby ascertained she was in fact living in the back kitchen with the old lady. The door was locked and Mary Ann said she had not got the key and had not seen Mrs Stowell since the previous day. PC Battersby banged on the door and called out but there was no reply. Mary Ann told him she would not answer because she was 'as deaf as a post'. They walked round to a courtyard to look for an alternative means of entry when Mary Ann suddenly made a break for it and tried to clamber over an eight-foot-high garden wall. PC Battersby summoned assistance with his whistle and PC Jackson took charge of the prisoner while he gained entry to the kitchen through a window.

There, lying with her head in the fire grate, her neck resting on the fender, was the battered body of 78-year-old Mary Stowell. She was bleeding from a head wound and her ribcage was smashed in. A heavy poker was lying next to the body. She had also been strangled with a rope, which had been wrapped six times round her neck and was still knotted tightly.

The bundles in the hall were found to contain Mrs Stowell's clothing, marked with her initials 'M.S.' Mary Ann's clothing was bloodstained and the victim's jewellery was found her in her pockets. In a last desperate bid to escape justice, Mary Ann first tried to bribe PC Battersby with 20 shillings to let her go, and then tried to strangle herself with her gown after asking to use the water closet.

Mary Ann Hunt was arrested for the murder but denied all knowledge about how her old friend had met her death. The attractive 30-year-old servant appeared at the Marylebone Police Courts later that day without an apparent care in the world and pleaded not guilty. She was mobbed by a hostile crowd, who hissed and jeered as she was driven away to Newgate Prison.

At the inquest on Friday 4 June at the nearby Carpenter's Arms, neighbours reported that the pair frequently quarrelled and Mary Ann was often heard shouting threats. Mrs Stowell had also recently told her daughter that she wanted her lodger out of the house as she was frightened of being killed by her.

Mary Ann believed that the old lady was a miser and had plenty of money hidden in the kitchen drawer, and had refused to pay the 'covetous old wretch' any rent. Mr Moat, the police surgeon, gave evidence that the murderer had tried to strangle the deceased with the rope but, being unsuccessful, had knocked her down with the poker and then tried to manually strangle her before jumping on her chest several times, breaking ten ribs and rupturing her right lung, which led to her death.

The jury returned a verdict of wilful murder against Mary Ann Hunt and she was committed for trial. On Thursday 19 August 1847 the trial opened at the Old Bailey. The evidence against her was overwhelming and she could no longer deny her involvement. Instead her defence was that she was in a disturbed state of mind and was prone to fits and therefore could not be responsible for her actions.

The jury took 25 minutes to decide her guilt but recommended mercy on account of her previous good character. Mr Justice Erle was not so forgiving and, donning his black cap, told the prisoner the crime was so dreadful that she could not hold out any hope of commutation. Mary Ann, who was apparently completely unmoved by the drama of proceedings, had another card up her sleeve, however. She loudly announced that she was pregnant by an officer of the Metropolitan Police Detective Squad, who, failing to send her money as promised, drove her to desperate measures which culminated in murder. The judge, somewhat taken aback, ordered her to be examined by a 'jury of matrons'.

Whilst in prison awaiting examination, Mary Ann admitted that after being repeatedly pressed for rent, she killed Mrs Stowell in a fit of temper. She forced open the kitchen drawer only to find it contained just 20 shillings, which she took with the old woman's belongings and fled to the railway station to catch a train to Brighton. The last train had departed, however, and so Mary Ann returned to the house and remained with the body until the early hours, at which point she was apprehended by the vigilant PC Battersby.

Bryanstone Square

When she was finally examined by the 'jury of matrons', they initially concluded that she was not pregnant and should not be spared. However, a subsequent doctor's examination confirmed that she was indeed five months pregnant and she gave birth to a baby boy two months later. She remained in Tothill Fields Prison until the child was two years old, when mother and child were both transported for life to Australia, thereby escaping the hangman's noose for her callous crime.

THE MURDEROUS HOUSEKEEPER OF HARLEY STREET

SARAH DRAKE 1849

ON BOXING DAY 1844 A SMALL TRUNK WAS DELIVERED TO THE HOME OF THEOPHILUS BURTON AT NORTH LEVERTON NEAR RETFORD, NOTTINGHAMSHIRE. THE VILLAGE BLACKSMITH AND HIS WIFE, MARY, WERE INTRIGUED TO SEE THAT THE UNEXPECTED GIFT HAD BEEN SENT VIA TRAIN AND COACH FROM EUSTON RAILWAY STATION IN LONDON.

Their excitement was short-lived, however. As they opened the lid of the trunk they were horrified to discover the dead body of a newborn child. The post-mortem revealed the infant had probably been born dead and delivered by its mother. Enquiries in London proved fruitless and the baby was buried locally after an open verdict at the inquest.

Five years later, on Saturday 30 November 1849, Mary Burton received a letter from her elder sister Sarah Drake, who was in service in London, to say that she had sent her a parcel. It was to be delivered to the White Hart Inn in Retford. It was collected the following morning by her brother William Drake, who picked up the heavy box and carried it the mile or so home, on his shoulders. He noticed it bore a label addressed to: 'Mr Theophilus Burton, North Leverton, near Retford, Notts.', and thinking this was no longer needed, tore it off on the way home.

Upon delivering it to his sister's house, he and his brother-in-law Theophilus forced open the lock with a chisel and found it contained the body of a dead boy, wrapped in a bundle of clothing. PC Edward Smith arrived on the scene and summoned Dr Francis Blagg. The surgeon ascertained that the child was about two years of age and had not been dead for many days. The child was naked apart from a white pocket handkerchief around his neck. There were black bruises on the left temple and left ear a little bigger than a halfpenny, which had been inflicted with severe force by a blunt instrument. There were also compression marks around the throat. It was the doctor's opinion that either the strangulation or the head injuries were capable of causing the child's death.

Also in the box was an apron bearing the name 'S. Drake', written in black ink. Superintendent Thomas Kinder took charge of the case. He retrieved the discarded luggage label on the turnpike road and ascertained that the trunk had been sent by the London and North West Railway from Euston on 29 November by Sarah Drake from 33 Upper Harley Street, London.

Harley Street

Kinder contacted Scotland Yard and Detective Sergeant Whicher, who was later to find fame in the case of Constance Kent, arranged to meet him in London to conduct a joint enquiry. On Friday 7 December the officers went to 33 Upper Harley Street, where they found the housekeeper Sarah Drake and arrested her for the murder of her child. She looked at them in astonishment and said, 'How do you know that?' She was told her apron had been found with the body, whereupon she collapsed and began to sob. Whicher searched the housekeeper's cupboard and found three more aprons in a cupboard identically marked 'S. Drake' in black ink.

The murder trial began on Thursday 10 January 1850 at the Old Bailey. Drake looked sickly, emaciated and agitated and appeared much older than her 36 years. She covered her face with a handkerchief throughout the trial, was bent over double and could barely stand to make her not guilty plea.

The court heard that Sarah Drake had been a servant at Tusmore House near Bicester in 1845 until July 1847, when she left after falling pregnant by a French butler called Louis Taverne in the same household. Her son, also called Louis, was born on 9 October 1847. In January 1848, unable to look after the illegitimate child, she gave it to a childminder called Jane Johnson, a policeman's wife in Peckham. She agreed to pay six shillings a week for his keep and told her to bring him up as her own. However, after three months the payments became few and far between and Mrs Johnson received several letters pleading poverty and illness or telling of imminent departures to exotic climes. There were very few visits to the child and when the boy was taken ill in June 1848, the doctor advised her to baptise the child as he feared it might die. The mother's whereabouts were unknown but the child recovered. The Johnsons felt they had been left literally holding the baby and had received no payment for months.

In February 1849 Sarah Drake turned up out of the blue and announced that she would be taking the child to Boulogne, where his father was raised. Mrs Johnson accompanied Sarah Drake to Croydon railway station, where she bought a ticket to Dover. Mrs Johnson bade the child farewell, but the next evening Sarah Drake turned up back on her doorstep with little Louis and told her that a doctor had diagnosed the child with water on the brain and that he was unlikely to survive. She then left Louis with Mrs Johnson again, agreeing to pay her five shillings a week for his keep.

PC Henry Johnson was posted from Peckham to Shirley Common and he and his wife took Louis with them to their new home. The child was in good health but before long the payments stopped and were soon £9 in arrears. Henry put his foot down and said this arrangement could not be allowed to continue, and the child must be returned to Sarah Drake.

On Monday 26 November 1849 Drake wrote to Mrs Johnston pleading extreme poverty, saying she was ill but was going to Madrid with a family on a wage of £15 a year; if she survived she would do what she could, and if she died she would cause her clothes to be sold to discharge the debt. This was complete fabrication and in fact that day she had secured a job as a housekeeper to wealthy merchant banker Frederick Huth of Upper Harley Street, at a wage of £50 per year.

On the morning of Wednesday 28 November Mrs Johnson took baby Louis to 33 Upper Harley Street and confronted Drake with her lies. Sarah urged Mrs

Johnson to keep the child for a week longer but she refused, telling her that she must take the child back immediately and settle the outstanding debt, otherwise her husband would begin legal proceedings. Little Louis was taken to the housekeeper's room in the basement, where he was handed over to his mother. She remarked on how well the 'hearty fellow' looked.

This was the last time he was seen alive. Within minutes of Mrs Johnson's departure, Drake killed the child by hanging him and beating him around the head with a heavy object. She then packed the little body into a trunk and told one of the housemaids, Mary Anne Wignell, that she wanted to send some items to her sister and asked her to carry it down to the butler's pantry. It was so heavy, she later testified, that she could barely carry it. The following morning Drake arranged for the unsuspecting footman William Bryan to take the makeshift coffin to Euston Square station and put it on the train to North Leverton.

After her arrest, Sarah Drake made an unsolicited confession to a woman gaoler. She said, 'It's all about a child. I was afraid of losing my place. I hung the child – I did it in a moment. I packed it up and sent it to my sister. I imagine I will hang for it.'

DS Whicher carried out the investigation with his usual thoroughness. He was convinced that she had murdered the earlier illegitimate child which had been sent to her sister in 1844, but was unable to prove it. He did, however, make the astounding discovery that Sarah Drake had served time in prison following the discovery of a third child that had been killed and boxed up in an identical manner to little Louis.

On 15 April 1842 the Knutsford Union Workhouse in Cheshire received a wooden box containing the dead body of a newborn male child. It had been addressed to Mr Joseph Tipley, the workhouse porter, and contained a cryptic note which read, 'You would be doing your wife a favour if you bury this'.

This child had been born alive and had been strangled shortly after birth. Finger marks were clearly visible around the child's throat. Enquiries revealed the box had been posted from Euston Square station and the investigations led back to Sarah Drake, who at that time was employed as a cook at the home of a Leyton magistrate.

Fellow servants reported that on 6 April 1842, Drake was confined to bed with a swollen stomach. She emerged three days later saying that she had a tumour which had now burst and she was feeling much better. On 13 April she asked a maid to lend her a box as she wanted to send some belongings to her family in the country. The laundry woman later noticed blood-soaked bedding and under-garments stained with discharges of milk, which led colleagues to conclude that she had given birth.

Drake was tried for murder at the Old Bailey on Tuesday 10 May 1842. She appeared before the court in a pitiful state, denying having killed the child and stating the child had been stillborn and she did not know what to do with it. Her performance clearly had the desired effect on the jury, who instead of murder found her guilty of the much lesser offence of concealment of birth, for which she was sentenced to six months' imprisonment.

Eight years later, on Thursday 10 January 1850, in an almost identical re-enactment, Sarah Drake again found herself in the dock at the Old Bailey charged with the murder of little Louis. This time she pleaded temporary insanity, claiming she could not distinguish right from wrong. Incredibly the jury accepted the plea and, despite a complete absence of medical evidence to support the claim, she was judged unfit to plead and declared insane, to be detained at Her Majesty's pleasure at Bethlem Hospital. She was transferred shortly afterwards to Brixton Prison, where she successfully secured her release at the end of 1857 after serving just seven years. She returned to live with her parents in North Leverton, where in 1891 she died, a blind old woman, at the age of 77, having escaped the hangman's noose three times over.

THE SLAUGHTER OF THE LAMBETH SERVANT

ANN MARIA MARTIN 1880

ANN MARIA MARTIN WAS A 55-YEAR-OLD SPINSTER WHO RAN A LODGING HOUSE AT 7 YORK ROAD, LAMBETH. MISS MARTIN, A FORMER COOK, HAD A REPUTATION AS A FORCEFUL WOMAN. SHE WAS VERY MASCULINE IN BOTH HER APPEARANCE AND HER MANNER. SHE EMPLOYED 17-YEAR-OLD ORPHAN ELIZA BARLOW AS HER MAID OF ALL WORK.

By June 1880, Eliza had worked for her demanding mistress for 3½ years and knew her strange ways very well. Eliza had previously suffered fits and her mistress would not allow her to leave the house alone. As a result, her only surviving relative, her uncle James Bottley, rarely saw her, despite living just a few hundred yards away. Miss Martin's eccentric behaviour brought her into regular conflict with her neighbours, whom she frequently accused of spying on her. No one realised that her paranoia was a symptom of rapidly declining mental health.

On Tuesday morning, 22 June, Miss Martin and Eliza left the house to go shopping. As they passed the local policeman, PC Josland, Miss Martin asked him if he had heard the thunder the night before. Eliza quietly quipped, '… and the missus is looking as black as thunder too this morning – is she not, policeman?'

The following day neighbours thought it odd that the shutters remained closed and there was no sign of life at the house, so they alerted Miss Martin's brother George who called round to see her. During his visit he saw Eliza busy in the kitchen and noticed that his sister was behaving oddly towards her, at one point interrupting him in mid-conversation, saying, 'Stop – the girl is listening.' George put this down to the 'problems with her head', from which his sister had recently suffered.

At 6pm, her brother called again but was unable to persuade her to admit him. He returned at 9am the next day to see if she would answer the door to the milkman, but she did not.

That evening he called again and this time his sister opened the door a fraction on the security chain and said, 'You are not my brother George. Go away! I do not know your voice.' He asked her to open the door and take in the milk can which had been hanging on the railing all day. She did so reluctantly, but still refused to let him in.

Later that evening George called for his elder brother

James and both went to see their sister. They managed to gain access to the house, but were immediately set upon by their sister, who attacked them with her fists screaming hysterically, 'You are the people who are coming after me and I have done for one already.' They managed to restrain her in a chair but were suspicious about what she might have done. After calming her down they went to the kitchen, where they found it in a state of disarray. There was blood on the floor and on the table; and ominously no sign of young Eliza.

Fearing something was amiss; they went to Kennington Road police station and returned to the house with Sergeant Jupe. Again they were attacked with such force by the old woman that she had to be locked in the parlour while reinforcements were summoned.

Victorian London

Once she had been restrained the police officers began to search the house. In the kitchen they recoiled in horror when their lamps illuminated a small trunk measuring 26 by 15 inches and little over a foot high. Wedged grotesquely in the box was the body of the petite servant girl. The body, which had been folded double and forced into the box, was still warm to the touch. Her head had been sawn off and had been crudely stuffed between her legs in her wooden tomb. Her skull bore signs of severe blunt force trauma, including an injury 2½ inches wide and 1½ inches deep on the right side of her forehead. It was estimated that she had been dead for between ten and twelve hours. No attempt had been made to conceal the body.

There was evidence that the surfaces had been washed down and the floor mopped, although in the scullery the police found fresh blood upon which quicklime had been sprinkled. A bloody meat saw was found nearby and a bloodstained bed upon which the awful beheading had taken place. In the back room, the murder weapon, a blood-soaked hammer, was found lying on a fender.

Ann Maria Martin was arrested and charged with the wilful murder of her maidservant. She denied all responsibility. On 5 August 1880 she appeared at the Old Bailey where the Newgate prison surgeon declared her insane and unfit to plead. She was ordered to be detained during Her Majesty's pleasure and was sent to Broadmoor criminal lunatic asylum in Berkshire, where she died on 22 March 1895 at the age of 71. She left her brother James £2,321, the equivalent of £200,000 by today's standards.

THE ISLINGTON OUTRAGES

ALFRED GAMBLE 1895

DURING LATE 1895, LONDON WAS SHOCKED BY THE ABDUCTION AND MURDER OF A CHILD IN BROAD DAYLIGHT JUST YARDS FROM THE BUSY AGRICULTURAL HALL IN ISLINGTON, NOW THE BUSINESS DESIGN CENTRE.

On Thursday morning, 10 October 1895, Mrs Ellen Dowling of 40 Parkfield Street, Islington, washed and dressed her 2¼-year-old son Sidney Victor and took him across the road to Mrs Murphy's general store to get some provisions. She returned home and left Sidney on the doorstep eating a handful of dates while she went inside. She checked on him a few moments later and found that someone had given him a bruised pear. She cut away the discoloured portion and left him eating the fruit. Sidney was a pretty and popular little boy and it was usual for him to sit on the step watching the world go by while his mother was busy with the morning's chores. After 20 minutes, his mother called him and was surprised to receive no reply. She went outside and found that he had gone. She began frantically searching the busy streets but there was no sign of him.

At the same time a young servant, Harriet Willoughby, living next door at number 41 Parkfield Street, heard a thump on the dustbin in the rear yard. Thinking it was local lads messing about, she went to see what was going on. She saw that a sack had been thrown on top of the dustbin with what she thought was the head of a wax doll protruding from it. As she touched it, she felt it was warm and screamed out in horror as she realised it was the body of a dead child. Paper had been stuffed down the throat of little Sidney, and he had suffocated. Doctors tried for 45 minutes to resuscitate the toddler but to no avail.

At 1pm police conducting house to house enquiries discovered the dead child's clothing wrapped in newspaper in the tiny six-foot-square yard of number 42, belonging to local greengrocer Mary Burgess. Her disabled brother Joseph Manston collapsed with shock, exclaiming, 'Good God, I am innocent!' as the police arrested him for murder. Little Sidney's cap was found hanging on a hook in the house, and the sack in which his body was found was also identical to others found at the house.

Mercifully 'Hoppy Joe', as he was known, was able to prove he had been elsewhere at the time of the crime and Mrs Burgess admitted hanging up the cap after finding it in the house. Suspicion then began to fall on one of her barrow boys Alfred Gamble, who was the only other person with access to the house at the time of the murder.

Gamble was a tall, thin, sallow 16-year-old known locally as 'Chopper'. He had been working on his barrow in nearby Chapel Street at the time of the murder and had been seen giving a pear to Sidney Dowling while he was sitting on his doorstep. Mrs Dowling also knew the youth, having six months previously accused him of stealing her watch, which had caused ill-feeling between them.

Police arrested him at his home at 5 Oakley Place, St George's Road, Holloway and charged him with the murder of Sidney Dowling. He protested his innocence, saying; 'I ain't done nothing at all. I only gave him a pear. I didn't do anything of the kind. I wouldn't do a thing like that.'

Other cases then began to emerge of children mysteriously mutilated in Islington. Just days before the murder and barely 200 yards away, a baby boy left to play on the steps by its mother later crawled into the house in great agony. It was discovered that a portion of the child's stomach had been cut away.

A similar case of child mutilation had been reported in November 1894 by Mr and Mrs James Smith, who lived in the Quinn Buildings, Popham Street, Essex Road. One Sunday evening, the couple went for a stroll, leaving their two daughters, aged thirteen and nine, in bed. In an adjoining room was their baby boy, Willie. As they left, they saw Alfred Gamble, who lived in the same building, loitering in the hall. When the parents returned they found Willie was bleeding profusely from a horrific wound to his lower abdomen. Emergency treatment at St Bartholomew's saved his life, but he spent the next three months in hospital. Mrs Smith was told by a neighbour's boy that he had seen Gamble climbing out of her bedroom window just before they had returned home. The police, however, were not overly concerned by the incident at the time.

For the murder of Sidney Dowling, the police were satisfied that the case against Gamble was sound, but events took an unexpected turn when on Friday 25 October the case collapsed in court when he was discharged on the basis of insufficient evidence and lack of motive. 'Chopper' Gamble was back on the streets of Islington.

At 4.15pm on Tuesday 3 December, three-year-old William Charles Cattle went missing whilst

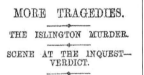

MORE TRAGEDIES.

THE ISLINGTON MURDER.

SCENE AT THE INQUEST— VERDICT.

On Monday the Coroner for North London opened an inquest on the body of Sidney Victor Dowling, aged two years, who was found murdered two doors away from his parents' house in Parkfield-street, Islington, on the previous Thursday under remarkable circumstances. There was a great crowd of women round the Coroner's Court. The boy, Alfred Gamble, who stands remanded at the police court on the charge of murder, was present. Evidence of identification was first given by the boy's mother. While Mrs. Dowling was giving her evidence her husband suddenly became hysterical, and a painful scene ensued as he was carried out of court by half a dozen officers, uttering heartrending

SIDNEY VICTOR DOWLING.

Newspaper Cutting of October 1895

playing in the road in Sidney Street, Goswell Road. His parents, costermongers Emily and Edward Cattle, searched frantically for him. At 6.45pm a carriage proprietor heard a piteous cry coming from the stables at 18 Sydney Grove, also owned by Gamble's' employer, Mrs Burgess. He found a caretaker and, with costermonger William Sharp, broke in. They struck a light and followed the sounds of whimpering to a corner of the stable where, hidden beneath a pile of greengrocer's baskets, they found a sack tied up tightly with cord. William Sharp cut open the sack with his pocket knife and found the blood-drenched body of Willie Cattle stuffed head first into the sack. His mouth was full of chaff and mud. His head was badly bruised, he had two stab wounds on his back and chest and his body had been frightfully mutilated. Miraculously he was still alive and was rushed to St Bart's Hospital.

William Sharp told detectives he had seen Alfred Gamble locking up the stable doors and walking away between four and five o'clock. A seven-year-old girl, Caroline Robinson, told police that Gamble had attempted to drag her into the same stable where Willie Cattell was later discovered. He had beaten her with a whip, but she had struggled violently and managed to escape from him.

At 7pm the next day Gamble was arrested by detectives at Mrs Burgess's greengrocery stall in Castle Street.

He denied having been near the stables the previous day although enquiries revealed that Mrs Burgess had sent Gamble to the stable to collect some sacks during the afternoon and he was missing for 1½ hours, not returning until 5pm. When she scolded him, he told her he had been sweeping out the stable.

George Irons, who was also employed by Mrs Burgess, said that at midday on the day of the crime, Gamble borrowed a pocket knife from him and had it sharpened by an Italian street grinder. Another witness reported seeing Gamble with Willie Cattle prior to his abduction. Gamble's own mother admitted that her son had been 'queer in the head for ten years' and was affected by the full moon.

At Old Street police station Gamble was charged with attempted murder but continued to protest his innocence, claiming there was a glass roof in the stable through which anyone could have entered if they lifted the glass.

On this indictment the evidence against Alfred Gamble finally seemed watertight, but again he managed to escape the hangman's noose. On Wednesday 15 January 1896 at the Old Bailey he appeared before Mr Justice Hawkins. He appeared to be deaf and when asked to plead replied, 'Not guilty', then muttered, 'The Inspector told me I had killed the boy in the stable.'

Doctors from Holloway Prison gave evidence to the effect that they believed he was congenitally imbecilic and not fit to plead, or even to understand the nature of the act charged. They considered he may have been epileptic and could have carried out the crimes during a fit, and then remembered nothing of them. Gamble was declared insane and unfit to stand trial, and was ordered to be detained indefinitely at Her Majesty's pleasure.

The families of the victims, who believed he was a cunning predator, felt that they had once more been denied justice. Thankfully Gamble was never freed to kill again and spent the following six decades of his life incarcerated in the asylum for the criminally insane in Surrey, dying in 1954 at the age of 75.

THE KENSINGTON RIPPER

REGINALD TRAHERNE BASSET SAUNDERSON 1894

DURING THE WINTER OF 1894, POLITE LONDON SOCIETY WAS SHAKEN BY THE ARREST OF A MEMBER OF THE PRIVILEGED CLASSES FOR THE SHOCKING MURDER OF A PRETTY YOUNG WOMAN IN A SMART KENSINGTON STREET, YARDS FROM THE HOME OF LORD LEIGHTON, THE PRESIDENT OF THE ROYAL ACADEMY.

At midnight on Sunday 25 November 1894, Herbert Schmalz, on his way to post a letter, saw a young couple struggling outside number 1 (now 10) Holland Park Road, the home of artist Valentine Prinsep. He heard the woman cry out 'Oh Christ!' and saw the man knee her in the stomach and draw his hand across her throat. As the woman fell to the floor Schmalz, not realising she had been mortally wounded, picked up a stick and chased her athletic assailant but lost him in Kensington High Street.

Meanwhile Herman Sauber, collecting his daughter from an artists' gathering, saw a figure lying in the gutter which he assumed was a drunk. He called out and, on receiving no reply, drew closer and was horrified to see the body of a young woman lying in a pool of blood. He raised the alarm and within minutes PC Thomas Gordon and PC William Paterson arrived on the scene. From the light of their lamps a yawning gash, which had severed the jugular vein, was clearly visible beneath the young woman's fur boa. Next to the body the murderer had dropped a distinctive cherrywood cane with a twisted handle.

The victim was 28-year-old barmaid Augusta Dawes, also known as Gus Dudley, who had moved to London from Bristol after the death of her once-affluent parents had left her penniless. She had beautiful striking features, large eyes and a dark complexion and soon became popular with the opposite sex. Within a few years she had two children out of wedlock. A promising relationship with a gentleman with a house on Fulham Palace Road ended abruptly when he was sentenced to ten years' imprisonment for fraud, and Augusta was turned out onto the streets.

Homeless and destitute, she was forced to leave her eldest son in the workhouse and descended into a spiral of despair, seeking solace in the demon drink. In the summer of 1894 she and her youngest daughter began to lodge with Lilian Creber at 36 St Clement's Road, Notting Dale. Miss Creber looked after the three-year-old while her mother went out to work at

The Holland Arms in Kensington High Street.

The Holland Arms

At 8pm on Sunday night, Augusta Dawes kissed her daughter Amy on the cheek for the last time. She set off into the cold night air sober and in good spirits, sporting a pretty bonnet and a distinctive fur boa, promising that she would be back as usual by midnight. When 1am came and she had still not returned, Lilian Creber knew there was something seriously wrong and she spent a sleepless night frantic with worry. The morning's headlines confirmed her worst fears – 'Bloody Murder in Kensington'. Lilian Creber rushed to the mortuary with Amy in her arms, where she identified the murdered body of her friend. The distraught child was reported to have held out her arms and cried out 'Mama, Mama.'

The post-mortem examination revealed a four-inch-long gash on the side of the victim's throat, just below her left ear. The ferocious wound, almost three inches deep, had been inflicted with such force that it had snagged the vertebrae. There were also finger marks from a left hand on her neck, indicative of partial strangulation.

A huge manhunt was mounted for the 'Kensington Ripper'. On Monday morning, 500 yards from the scene of the crime, D/Sgt Thompson found the murder weapon, a peculiar Swedish Slojde knife, stuck into a wooden scaffold pole.

Despite extensive enquiries Scotland Yard was baffled by the motiveless murder, until a breakthrough arrived via the Royal Mail. On Wednesday 28 November an extraordinary letter arrived at Knightsbridge Police Station, posted the day before in Dublin. Detectives were initially sceptical of the letter, signed by 'Jack the Ripper'; however, it contained a plan of the crime scene and a detailed description of where the knife had been discarded, details which could have only been known to the killer.

Dublin, Nov. 27th

Dear Sir, The murder that was committed I did it. I did it just to the right of the door of a gentleman. I got her by the throat and tried to choke her, but without success. I got her on the ground and cut her ... with a sloid knife. It was a very good cut. When I had cut her a fellow was coming along, so I flew for my life, but left the stick, and the knife was thrown away in the back lane in a back street. I did the murder at 12-30. So goodbye. On the job. From Jack the Ripper. You will find my name is well known at certain places round there. I am now at ------.

Crucially 'Jack' provided an address where he could be found in Ireland. At the same time, police received reports from the Hampton Wick asylum of Dr Langdon Down, who is famous for identifying Down's syndrome. He reported that one of his more troublesome residents was missing and had taken with him a knife and a cherrywood walking cane.

Detectives raced to Hampton Wick with the Irish letter, where the handwriting was identified as that of the missing patient, Reginald Traherne Basset Saunderson, who had just celebrated his 21st birthday. Saunderson was a member of the Irish landed gentry, the nephew of a prominent MP and could trace his lineage back to 'Bloody' Mary. In December 1888 he had been placed in the full-time care of Dr Down, having sustained a head injury in childhood.

On the evening of the murder, Saunderson had made his way into London where at 10pm he called at Eliza Ahrens' boarding house at St Alban's Place in the Haymarket and asked for a room for the night, saying he was ill with rheumatic fever. Fortunately perhaps for her, Mrs Ahrens had no vacancies that night; less than two hours later he was slitting the throat of Augusta Dawes. After fleeing the scene, he walked through the night to Harrow where he arrived for breakfast at the home his old schoolmaster Mr Davidson.

Saunderson told him that he had ridden there from Portsmouth but had had his bike stolen in Willesden. He explained away his bloodstained gloves by saying he had helped a policeman lift up the body of a murdered girl whose throat had been cut at Westminster Bridge. He borrowed a sovereign on the pretext of going back to Portsmouth, but had in fact booked a passage to Dublin, heading for his ancestral home at Castle Saunderson at Belturbet. On Tuesday 27 November, after trying unsuccessfully to enlist in the army at Linenhall Barracks, Dublin, he posted his 'Jack the Ripper' letter.

On 3 December Saunderson was arrested at the home of Mrs Jones at Belturbet. In his possession were two newspaper cuttings relating to the murder. He was collected by Detective Sergeants Thompson and Dyson from the Metropolitan Police CID. After taking breakfast and being medicated for a cough, he thanked the Irish police for their kindness and was escorted to the railway station and boarded a specially reserved first-class carriage to Dublin. During the crossing to Holyhead aboard LNWR boat Banshee he was observed chatting and smoking with the detectives, without handcuffs, in the saloon below deck.

Back at Willesden Junction a sizeable crowd had gathered at the railway station to catch a glimpse of the 'Kensington Ripper'. Dressed in a hard black felt hat, an ulster overcoat and a cape, Saunderson stepped off the train looking 'pallid, haggard and fatigued'. Although youthful in appearance, with a faint outline of a moustache, he was broad shouldered and, at six foot, was taller than his custodians.

He was remanded to Holloway gaol, where his wealthy family ensured that his privileged treatment continued. He was excused cell-cleaning duties and allowed luxuries denied to other prisoners such as carpets and a feather bed. He was, however, put on a twenty-four-hour suicide watch.

After committal to the Old Bailey, his father Llewellyn Saunderson gave evidence that his son was an imbecile and incapable of understanding the consequences of his actions. The court was told that his condition had deteriorated while in custody and that he had to be confined to a padded cell for his own protection and that of others. Saunderson told doctors that he heard voices in his head urging him to do violent acts.

Four doctors unanimously agreed that he was insane and unfit to face trial. He was sentenced to be detained at Her Majesty's pleasure and on 30 January 1895 he was sent to Broadmoor Hospital for the Criminally Insane.

There has been much speculation about whether or not Reginald Saunderson could have been Jack the Ripper. As a powerful and athletic six-footer he had the capability, but most Ripperologists agree, that as he was only fifteen years old at the time, he is an unlikely suspect for the Whitechapel murders. It is more likely that he was inspired by the notorious serial killer and that Augusta Dawes became the tragic victim of his murderous fantasies. He died in Broadmoor in 1943 at the age of 70.

Police Surgeon Dr James Maughan found that the front of the skull had been crushed with a heavy blow and there was evidence that he had still been alive when he was placed into the oven. There was blood and hair on a hatchet which lay nearby, and bloodstains and brain tissue splashed on the wall and dough trough where he had been attacked. Detectives searching Berndt's room found in his jacket pocket a receipt for a pocket watch he had recently bought, but the watch and chain could not be found.

Meanwhile two police officers on night patrol in the Hampstead Road spotted a suspicious figure, walking breathlessly towards George Street. Constables Albert Hern and Jeremiah Westcot called out to him but he threw something down and bolted. The officers gave chase and brought him to the ground outside Euston Square railway station, and when they retraced his route they found he had discarded a bloodstained folding knife. He denied any knowledge of the weapon but they noticed he had a bloodstain on his cuff and recent burns to his hands, and arrested him on suspicion.

At the police station, news was coming in about the atrocity at the bakehouse, and the foreign prisoner in the cell block perfectly fitted the description of the wanted man. He denied being Richard Montague and identified himself as Johann Schneider. On being searched, a silver pocket watch and chain was found in his breast coat pocket, which he claimed he had owned for two years. It was found to bear the same serial number as the receipt in Berndt's jacket pocket. A piece of paper torn from the bakery notebook bearing his address was also found in his pocket.

Any doubt was removed when William Ross came to the police station and positively identified the prisoner as the man he knew as Richard Montague. After being charged with murder, Schneider continued to protest his innocence, saying, 'I know nothing about it. I don't know that shop'.

At the inquest into the death of Conrad Berndt on Monday 14 November the Coroner heard that Berndt, also a German, was quiet, hardworking and trustworthy, and had worked as assistant baker to William Ross for six months. His body had been charred beyond recognition and even his aunt and uncle could not identify his remains. He was identified by his watch and chain. The jury returned a verdict of wilful murder by Johann Schneider, whose real name was Mandelknow.

At his Old Bailey trial, Schneider collapsed in the dock as the grisly evidence of Conrad's scorched cadaver was given by the traumatised police officers who had removed it from the oven. It was believed that, as was the usual practice, Conrad would have been napping next to the dough trough in between duties and that while he was asleep he was savagely struck on the temple with the hatchet, fracturing his skull in two places. He was then bundled into the oven. After committing the crime Schneider ransacked Conrad's bedroom and stole his watch and chain, and was hastily attempting to wash away evidence when he was interrupted by the arrival of Mr Ross.

The defence tried to enter a plea of insanity but the judge would hear none of it and the jury unanimously found him guilty of murder – committed for the sake of a pocket watch worth just £1. On 15 December 1898 the sentence of death was passed on him, translated into German in case he was left in any doubt as to his fate. On the morning of his execution, in a state of 'extreme terror', Schneider had to be dragged to the scaffold, where his last words were reported to be 'Jesus Christ, Forgive me all my wickedness and sins'.

Crowds flocked to the bakehouse to get a glimpse of the infamous oven, but trade was so badly affected by the gruesome crime that William Ross was forced to shut up shop and move to another premises nearby, helped by a donation from the Master Bakers' Protection Society, who also paid for the funeral of and memorial to young Conrad Berndt.

Within days of his execution Madame Tussauds had added Schneider's grim waxwork to their Chamber of Horrors, together with the very oven he used to commit the crime, bought from William Ross.

MURDER AT MILLER'S COURT, WHITECHAPEL

KATE MARSHALL 1898

DURING THE EARLY HOURS OF SUNDAY 27 NOVEMBER 1898, DORSET STREET, WHITECHAPEL, ONCE DUBBED 'THE WORST STREET IN LONDON', AGAIN ECHOED TO CRIES OF 'BLOODY MURDER!'.

Shortly after midnight PC Alfred Fry was patrolling the dark cobbled streets when he was alerted by distressing screams coming from the direction of Miller's Court. Turning the corner, his blood ran cold as he confronted the most notorious lodging house in London, where Mary Kelly had been brutally dismembered by Jack the Ripper almost ten years ago to the day. One of the many tenants of 26 Dorset Street was Charlie Amory, who was holding aloft a bloodstained knife and frantically pointing upstairs, where the sound of shrieks could be heard coming from the first floor.

As PC Fry bounded up the stairs he was confronted with a scene of carnage. There on the landing he found

David Roberts struggling to restrain a woman who was thrashing about wildly on the floor, screaming and biting. Lying nearby was the blood-soaked body of a young woman who had been stabbed in the chest, her dress drenched in a crimson, tide, flowing from a gaping wound under her right breast.

Reinforcements arrived and the violent, hysterical woman was handcuffed and taken to Commercial Road police station. She was 44-year-old Kate Marshall, the sister of the victim, and had recently been released from prison.

At the inquest the following day, the jury heard the full story unfold. The deceased was Lizzie Roberts (36), who had taken pity on her alcoholic sister Kate Marshall on seeing her poor state of health after her gaol term. She gave her lodgings at the squalid single-room tenement she shared with her husband and their three-year-old son. Although she was a difficult lodger, Lizzie helped her sister to make an honest living by selling toy whips around the streets and pubs of Whitechapel.

Her husband David Roberts explained that Saturday morning had begun innocently enough. At 7.30am he went out to his work as a painter and decorator, and when he returned to 26 Dorset Street at 6.30pm noticed with some relief that Kate Marshall was not at home. At 7.15pm his wife left the house in high spirits, saying she was going out to sell some whips.

By 10pm she had not returned home, so David and his young son went to bed. The room was less than nine feet square and consisted of a bed, which they had given over to their lodger, and, on the other side of a makeshift partition, a mattress on the floor on which David, Lizzie and their son slept.

At midnight he was awoken by the drunken revelry of his wife and sister coming home. They burst into the room worse the wear for drink, barely able to stand and carrying a quart can of ale. They poured David a glass of beer and began to regale him loudly with tales of what they had been doing that night. An argument then broke out between the two sisters over money. The row got worse as Lizzie accused her sister of being ungrateful for what she had done for her since her release from prison.

This sent Kate into a violent rage, and crockery was thrown and windows were smashed before David could intervene and restore order. For a few minutes all was quiet and David went back to bed to comfort his young son, who was understandably upset by the commotion. He then heard the sound of drunken laughter followed by a scuffle and Kate shouting, 'Is that what you mean?'

As David got to his feet he saw Kate rushing at his wife, shouting, 'You thing, I will give you something for this,' and she struck a blow at her chest. His wife cried out, 'Dave – she has stabbed me!' It was then that

David saw that Kate was brandishing the razor-sharp shoemaker's knife she had brought two days before, to cut the leather for the whips.

He grabbed her wrists but she resisted violently and they tumbled out through the door onto the landing. Unable to loosen her hands, David kicked the partition wall and shouted for help from his neighbour, Charlie Amory. He finally managed to prise the knife from her hand and pass it to his neighbour, as she tore his shirt to ribbons with her nails and sank her teeth into his arms. His wife, meanwhile, had collapsed on the landing, bleeding profusely from a two-inch-long wound to her left arm and a deep stab wound 'two fingers wide' beneath her heart.

Dr Hume was summoned and Lizzie's blood-drenched body was taken into Charlie Amory's room, where the surgeon administered brandy, but it was too late. Within minutes she died from severe blood loss in the very room where Mary Kelly had taken her last breath ten years before. Kate Marshall, seeing the corpse of her sister, cried out, 'Oh God, Oh God, what have I done, Liz? Let me see her. I must have a kiss before I die.'

The inquest jury had no hesitation in reaching a verdict of wilful murder and Kate Marshall was committed for trial. She appeared at the Old Bailey on Wednesday 11 January 1899, looking haggard and pale, but astonished the court by pleading not guilty and accusing her brother-in-law David Roberts of the murder of his wife. She claimed that she and her sister, with whom 'she had never had a cross word', had come home at 7pm to find David Roberts 'shocking drunk'. They left him to it and went out, returning together at midnight, when a disturbance had ensued in which he swore at them and accused them of not selling whips but 'selling something else'.

In a violent rage he had then jumped out of bed and attacked his wife. Kate had rushed to her aid, pulled David off her and struggled violently with him, ripping his shirt in the process, before falling out onto the landing just as the police arrived. This unlikely scenario caused a commotion in the jury box when it was disclosed that the doting husband had been bound over just a month before her death, for hitting his wife over the head with a poker in a drunken rage.

The prosecuting counsel Horace Avory then pulled out his trump card by asking Kate Marshall if she had stabbed anyone before. Immediately her defence objected in the strongest terms to this prejudicial line of questioning. After adjourning to consult with senior colleagues, Mr Justice Darling declared that the question was not unfair and evidence of her antecedents was admissible. When the trial resumed the jury listened wide-eyed as the grim tally of her previous convictions for violence was read out to the court.

MARCH 1879: Eight months' hard labour for cutting a woman's face with a broken plate

MAY 1883: Two months' hard labour for assaulting her sister Lizzie in a drunken attack

NOVEMBER 1883: Two months' hard labour for assault

OCTOBER 1884: Ten months' hard labour for maliciously wounding David Roberts' brother with a knife

APRIL 1890: Eighteen months' hard labour for stabbing

AUGUST 1894: Three months' hard labour for assault

Her most recent conviction, in May 1895, was five years' imprisonment for stabbing a former lover in the head after he refused to buy her a drink. He was lucky to survive the attack and spent the rest of his life with a silver plate in his skull. During her trial for this offence, the arresting officer, PC Thomas Masterman described her as 'One of the most dangerous women in the East End of London and a perfect terror to the neighbourhood'.

Defiant to the end, Kate Marshall dismissed her criminal history, claiming that all the assaults had been carried out in self-defence, and even accused David Roberts of having stabbed his brother although she had taken the blame. This string of convictions for violent assault removed any lingering doubts the jury may have had and, after just 25 minutes, they returned a unanimous verdict of guilty. They did, however, make a recommendation of mercy to the judge in the light of an absence of premeditation, and the fact that the crime was carried out 'in the frenzy of drink'.

Kate Marshall continued to protest her innocence as the sentence of death was passed on her, shouting; 'Oh Jesus this is perfect murder. Oh Dave Roberts has killed my sister. Where is God? I call upon Him'

As the wardens struggled to take her down to the cells she again violently resisted and screamed out; 'I am guilty of the other convictions. I have over twenty stabs myself and I say before Lord Jesus and the Trinity and Heaven, that I am innocent of this dreadful charge. God knows I am innocent and I call upon Him, my defender before the whole world. Do what you will with me but I am innocent!'

Kate Marshall was eventually spared the noose and her sentence was later commuted to penal servitude. She spent the rest of her life in prison, dying at Aylesbury gaol in Buckinghamshire in 1918 at the age of 63.

CARNAGE IN CAMBERWELL

EDGAR EDWARDS 1902

IN DECEMBER 1902 THE TRANQUILLITY OF A QUIET SUBURBAN STREET IN LEYTON, ESSEX WAS SHATTERED BY THE GRUESOME DISCOVERY OF THE DISMEMBERED REMAINS OF A YOUNG FAMILY BURIED IN A BACK GARDEN.

In November 1902, 34-year-old Edgar Edwards took over the tenancy of 89 Church Road, Leyton. Although he described himself as a grocer, he was in fact a petty criminal and had just been released from prison after serving five years for housebreaking.

Edwards employed a local jobbing gardener, Joseph Rawlings, to dig over the small back garden in order to plant flower beds. Neighbours watched the tall, smartly dressed, well-mannered man move his belongings into the house on a cart drawn by a black Shetland pony. They noticed that he had several large wooden crates, which he moved into the house with the help of a hunchbacked associate. They thought it odd when they saw him digging a hole so deep that his head was barely visible above ground, but by the following day the hole was filled in, so they thought little of it.

Edwards responded to an advert from a retired shopkeeper, John Garland, who was selling his shop near Victoria Park. On 22 December he invited him back home on the pretext of buying the business from him. Mr Garland arrived at midday and Edwards told him that he was waiting for some workmen to arrive, after which they would both go to Victoria Park to conclude the business. After four hours, with no sign of any workmen, Mr Garland said he needed to leave. As he placed his hand on the latch of the front door, he was struck an almighty blow from Edwards with a five-pound lead sash weight, which he had wrapped in a roll of music. Edwards rained down a flurry of savage blows until he was breathless from the effort but the old man, a former prize fighter, bravely resisted and his cries attracted the attention of a passing cabbie, who forced an entry and found the old man lying unconscious in a pool of blood.

When the police arrived, Edwards was calmly changing his blood-spattered shirt in the bedroom and claimed Garland had attacked him. He refused to give his name and was arrested for unlawful wounding.

While he was in custody, his landlord, Mr Basset, visited the house to query the false references he had been given and became suspicious about the extent of the digging that had taken place in the back garden. He alerted the police, who were anxious to discover the true identity of their uncooperative prisoner. On searching 89 Church

Road they discovered letters addressed to a Mr Darby at 22 Wyndham Road, Camberwell, and believing this could be their prisoner, they called at the address.

Detectives discovered that the previous tenants, William Darby (26), his pretty wife Beatrice (28) and their three-month-old daughter Eleanor had gone missing a month previously. A heavy lead weight, similar to the one with which old Mr Garland had been attacked, was also found in the house covered with blood and hair, together with two bloody saws. There were bloodstains on the bedroom wall and blood had seeped through the floorboards and was dripping through the ceiling below.

Police ascertained that their prisoner was Edgar Edwards, alias Alfred Joyce, who had spent most of his adult life in gaol. He had met and cold-bloodedly killed the hardworking young family just three days after being released from prison.

Just as he had later done with John Garland, Edwards had responded to an advertisement placed by William Darby offering the family business for sale. He met up with them at the Camberwell shop and, while agreeing to the sale, caught them off-guard and bludgeoned them in their own home. The bodies were left in the house for ten days while Edwards moved in, emptied the till, sold off their belongings and sub-let the shop to a former school friend, hunchback James Goodwin, warning him not to go upstairs as the Darbys' belongings were still there. Edwards then began to pass himself off as Darby and disposed of the shop stock, giving away bags of sweets to local children.

William and Beatrice Darby were last seen at their shop at 10pm on Saturday 29 November by their landlord, James Knight. When William Darby failed to keep an appointment, Knight called round to the shop and was shocked to see that Edwards had installed himself as proprietor, having allegedly bought the tenancy from Darby. The landlord was furious at the unauthorised transaction and threatened to call in the bailiffs. Fearing detection, Edwards cut up the bodies of the family and transported them in sacks to his new home in Church Road on a pony and trap, assisted by the hunchbacked Goodwin.

With clear evidence of murderous foul play, the police traced the sisters of the missing man, Mrs Baldwin and Mrs Kingswood, who were alarmed to hear of the sudden disappearance of their brother and went with the police to Church Road. There, they identified the furniture in Edwards' house as belonging to their missing brother. Even Beatrice Darby's wedding dress was found in the wardrobe. Glancing out of the bedroom window the sisters noticed a fresh mound of earth in the garden and Mrs Kingswood gasped, 'They must be buried out there!'

On 30 December, detectives began a search of the garden but were downhearted when their initial dig to a depth of two feet proved fruitless. However, Darby's pet black terrier, which had also been found at the house, began to paw at a particular spot in the garden. Spurred on by the dog's persistence, the police continued their excavations, and, some five feet below the surface, uncovered six coarse sacks and a bundle of blood-soaked clothing. When they were opened they caused even hardened detectives to recoil in horror. Stuffed into the sacks they found the mutilated body of William Darby; his head, legs and arms had been hacked off. His wife Beatrice had been similarly butchered and dismembered. In the final sack was the body of baby Eleanor, grotesquely entangled amongst the limbs of her mother.

Police surgeon Dr Jekyll conducted the post-mortem and concluded that the infant had been strangled with a handkerchief which was still tied tightly around her neck. The fractured skulls of the two parents indicated they had been killed by heavy blunt force trauma to the head. Their bodies had then been roughly sawn into eight parts.

Edwards continued to deny any knowledge of the decomposing bodies found in his garden, and when charged with the murders of the Darby family on New Year's Eve 1902 callously replied, 'My dear sir, I know nothing about it. Surely, sir, there is some great mistake!'

Edwards' behaviour throughout his Old Bailey trial was bizarre from the outset. A defence of insanity was dismissed by a panel of medical experts, and when asked for his plea he replied, 'You have no business to ask me such a question. What a load of nonsense'; and a not guilty plea was entered on his behalf.

After hearing the damning evidence the jury found no difficulty in finding Edwards guilty of murder. When asked if there was anything he wished to say, Edwards replied 'Right you are. Get on with it!' When the judge donned the black cap he was similarly contemptuous, shouting at him from the dock, 'Pass sentence as quickly as possible!' He left the court roaring with laughter and taunting his custodians with the words 'You'd better take good care of me – I'll get away if there's a ghost of a chance. You had trouble getting me out on Saturday morning – You'll have a damn sight harder time getting me out when I swing.'

In the event, on Tuesday 3 March 1903 he went quietly to the gallows but remained indifferent to the death sentence as he mounted the scaffold, sneering at the prison chaplain at Wandsworth Prison, 'I've been looking forward to this lot!' As the hangman, William Billington, placed the noose around his neck, he suddenly begged forgiveness as he was launched into eternity.

In a final theatrical gesture, Edwards left a letter to be opened after his death in which he claimed he was simply an accessory after the fact and named the alleged killer, possibly Goodwin. Police investigated his claims but charges were never brought against anyone else and this was considered to be the last cruel attempt of a callous and vicious killer to implicate another in his horrific crimes.

Edgar Edwards paid the ultimate price for his heinous crimes, and yet had he not spared the life of Darby's pet dog, this psychopathic killer might never have been brought to justice.

Oliver Twist pub in Church Road, Leyton, the local of murderer Edgar Edwards

BUTCHERY IN BARNET

BRIAN DONALD HUME 1947

'I, DONALD HUME, DO HEREBY CONFESS TO THE SUNDAY PICTORIAL THAT ON THE NIGHT OF OCTOBER 4, 1949, I MURDERED STANLEY SETTY IN MY FLAT IN FINCHLEY-ROAD, LONDON. I STABBED HIM TO DEATH WITH A DAGGER WHILE WE WERE FIGHTING'.

This remarkable confession created a sensation when it was published on the front page of the Sunday Pictorial on 1 June 1958 – and yet, to the frustration of the authorities, the killer could not be charged with murder. Brian Donald Hume had just been released after serving eight years in Dartmoor for being an accessory to the murder of car dealer Stanley Setty, but under the rules of double jeopardy in force at the time he could not be re-arrested for the same offence. Hume gloated to the world's press about butchering his victim and posed callously with the murder weapon, a Nazi dagger.

Hume had been an RAF pilot but was discharged in 1941 after being diagnosed with psychopathic tendencies.

During the war he posed as Dan Hume DFM and dropped forged cheques at Officer's Messes up and down the country. In the austere climate of shortages and rationing of post-war London, he made a comfortable living from smuggling and illegal activity around the motor trade. It was during this period that he began to do business with Stanley Setty, a Warren Street car dealer who had a prosperous lifestyle that Hume envied.

Brian Hume, allegedly paid £20,000 by the press for his confession

On 4 October 1949 Setty was reported missing and his car was found abandoned near his lock-up at St Pancras. He had just withdrawn £1,005 in £5 notes from the bank. On 21 October, a farm labourer named Stanley Tiffin was punting through the Essex marshes at Tillingham looking for ducks, when he discovered a parcel floating in shallow water. Thinking it might be of value he opened it and was horrified to discover the dismembered torso of a man, missing its head and legs. The body was identified by clothing and fingerprints as Stanley Setty. The post-mortem revealed that he had been killed by five stab wounds to the chest and there was impact damage to the body which suggested it had been dropped from a great height.

Enquiries at local airfields led the police to the United Services Flying Club in Elstree, where they ascertained that Hume, a club member, had hired a plane on 5th and 6th October and on both occasions had been seen to load large parcels into the co-pilot's seat. There was no incriminating evidence remaining in the Auster light aircraft, although there was some damage to the window consistent with something heavy having been pushed through it. Enquiries revealed Hume had paid for the plane and a taxi from the airfield from a roll of £5 notes, and the serial numbers proved they had been amongst those withdrawn from the bank by Setty on the day of his disappearance.

Hume was arrested and a search of his apartment in Golders Green, above a Finchley Road greengrocers, revealed heavy bloodstaining on the carpet, of the same group as the murdered man. The forensic evidence was consistent with Setty having been dismembered in the flat.

His charwoman, Ethel Stride, told police that on the day after the murder she noticed the front room carpet had gone. It transpired he had taken the carpet to a nearby cleaners and asked them to dye it from a pale green to a dark green. He offered her half a crown for a new floor cloth because he had ruined it 'cleaning stains from the carpet.' She also saw him carrying out suspiciously heavy brown paper parcels from the flat.

The circumstantial evidence against Hume mounted when it emerged the flamboyant 29-year-old company director was in deep financial trouble and owed money everywhere, but was able to clear his overdraft just days after the murder. He was later to claim that he had to burn most of the money as it was soaked with Setty's blood after the violent slaying.

Hume was charged with murder, but at his Old Bailey trial on 18 January 1950 he concocted a story that on 5 October, the day after Setty's disappearance, three gangsters called 'Mac', 'Greenie' and 'The Boy' had delivered two parcels to his flat and asked him to fly them out to sea and dump them, no questions asked. He believed they contained printing plates for forged petrol coupons. They paid him £150 in £5 notes. This parcel was flown out and dumped. When he returned, 'Mac' and 'The Boy' were waiting with another, larger parcel which he put in the kitchen cupboard.

The following day, 6 October, he got an employee to help him carry the heavy parcel out of the house and load it into a hired car. He later told police that, as they carried it, it made a gurgling noise. 'I thought it was a human body, that of a small man or a young person, and it crossed my mind that the package may have contained Setty's body as I had read in the papers that he was missing.'

In the first recorded case of a murderer disposing of his victim using an aeroplane, Hume headed for the Thames Estuary and jettisoned the body just off Southend, but he mistook the Essex marshes for open water and the dismembered body was washed up with the tide.

In January 1950, after retiring for 2½ hours, the jury announced that they could not reach a verdict on the capital charge. At the retrial an additional charge of being an accessory to murder was added to the indictment. Hume seized upon his chance to plead guilty to this lesser offence and was sentenced to twelve years' imprisonment.

He was released on good behaviour after serving just 8 years and gained worldwide notoriety after his high-profile and brazen confession. He fled to Switzerland in May 1958 on a false passport, where he quickly blew his fortune on a champagne lifestyle. Purporting to be a Canadian test pilot and anxious to maintain his playboy image, he embarked upon a series of bank robberies. Returning to Brentford in August 1958, he cold-bloodedly shot and wounded Midland Bank cashier Frank Lewis in the stomach before escaping back to Switzerland with £1,200. In November, he returned to the same branch, this time shooting the manager during a raid which netted him just £200.

In January 1959, having spent the night in a church drinking all their communion wine, he robbed a Zurich bank, shooting and injuring the cashier. He was chased by a taxi driver, whom he shot dead before being tackled by a plucky pastry cook when his gun jammed. His haul was just £17.

He was convicted of murder and sentenced to life imprisonment with hard labour. In August 1976 the Swiss authorities declared Hume to be insane and he was sent back to Britain and detained at Broadmoor.

In July 1998 a decomposing corpse was discovered in the grounds of the Copper Beeches Hotel in Basingstoke. Fingerprints confirmed the body to be 78-year-old Brian Donald Hume. The double killer had died of natural causes just weeks after his release.